EXCAVATING THE PAST

ANCIENT GREECE

Christine Hatt

Heinemann Library
Chicago, Illinois

Customer Service 888-454-2279
Visit our website at www.heinemannlibrary.com

Designed by Carole Binding
Originated by Ambassador Litho Ltd
Printed and bound in the United States by Lake Book
Manufacturing, Inc.

09 08 07 06
10 9 8 7 6 5 4 3 2

**Library of Congress Cataloging-
in-Publication Data**
A copy of the cataloging-in-publication data
for this title is on file with the Library of
Congress.
    Ancient Greece / Christine Hatt.
    ISBN 1-4034-4837-X (HC), 1-4034-
    5457-4 (Pbk.)

Acknowledgments
The author and publisher are grateful to the
following for permission to reproduce
photographs: pp. 5 bottom, 8, 10 top, 10 bottom,
11, 12, 13, 15 bottom, 20, 21, 22, 23 top, 23
bottom, 28, 29 top, 29 bottom, 30 top, 31, 32,
33, 34 top, 34 bottom, 35, 37, 38, 39, 40 Art
Archive; p. 6 Greek Ministry of Culture, Corbis/
Sygma; p. 9 bottom Berko Fine Paintings, Knokke-
Zoute, Belgium/Bridgeman Art Library; p. 10 top
Kevin Fleming/Corbis; pp. 14, 15 top, 26 Ancient
Art and Architecture Collection; p. 16, 30 bottom
British Museum, London/Bridgeman Art Library;
pp. 18, 19 The Johns Hopkins University; p. 24
top Donald A. Frey/Institute of Nautical
Archaeology; p. 24 bottom Institute of Nautical
Archaeology; p. 25 Jonathan Blair/Corbis; p. 27
Vince Streano/Corbis; p. 36 Index/Bridgeman
Art Library; p. 41 A. Dalton/TRIP; p. 42 John
Heseltine/Corbis; p. 43 Greek Ministry of Culture,
Corbis/Sygma.

Cover photograph of the ruins of the Temple of
Olympian Zeus reproduced with permission of
Corbis. Small photograph of the mask of Cronos
reproduced with permission of Werner Forman
Archive.

The publisher would like to thank Thorsten
Opper, of the British Museum (London), for
his help in the preparation of this book.

Some words are shown in bold, **like this.**
You can find out what they mean by
looking in the glossary.

CONTENTS

ARCHAEOLOGY AND THE ANCIENT GREEKS

Greece lies at the tip of the Balkan **Peninsula,** an area of southeast Europe that sticks out into the Mediterranean Sea. Humans have lived in this hot, dry land for more than 200,000 years, but the people now known as the ancient Greeks arrived much later. The first Greeks probably moved in from the north about 4,000 years ago. As more arrived, they spread south and, in a few hundred years, they had become the most powerful people in the region.

▽ *Over the last 200 years, **archaeologists** have investigated many ancient Greek **sites.** Their findings increase our understanding of how past peoples lived.*

The Greeks were different from the peoples already in the area in two main ways. They spoke a new language—Greek—and they believed in a group of gods who had not been heard of in the region before. The Greeks also introduced new styles of house-building and pottery-making.

Greeks through the ages

Experts divide ancient Greek history into different periods. The earliest period began in about 1600 B.C.E. By then, the Greeks had founded several rich kingdoms. One of the wealthiest was at Mycenae, so the period is called the Mycenaean Period.

● Sites described in this book

N

MACEDONIA — Pella
Vergina○
Olynthos
Mount Olympus ○

GREECE — Aegean Sea

Chaironeia
Delphi ○ ○ — EUBOIA
Thebes — Lefkandi
Plataia○
Marathon
Corinth○○ Isthmia○ — Athens Piraeus
○ Mycenae
○ Olympia — Epidaurus
PELOPONNESE PENINSULA
Sparta
○ Pylos

Mediterranean Sea

About 500 years later, after all its main sites were destroyed, the Mycenaean Period ended. Experts are not sure how or why this happened. Poverty and a decline in population followed, and so the next period, starting in 1100 B.C.E., is often known as the Dark Ages. However, recent research has shown that there were some strong communities in Greece during this period. Therefore many experts prefer to call it the Geometric Period, after the patterned pottery of the time.

From 750 B.C.E., the start of the Archaic Period, Greek cities and nearby villages began to form independent states. The largest was Athens. These **city-states** governed themselves, built temples, and encouraged the arts. From this time, the Greeks also set up **colonies** abroad.

The Classical Period

In 490 B.C.E., the Persian Empire tried to invade Greece and war followed as Athens, Sparta, and other city-states fought off the attackers. Eventually, after defeating the Persians in 479 B.C.E., the Greeks proudly started to rebuild. This was the start of the Classical Period, the high point of ancient Greek civilization.

△ *From Greece, it is easy to travel to other countries by sea. As the ancient Greeks grew stronger at home, they set up colonies around the Mediterranean and the Black Seas. They also traded with other lands.*

△ *This figure of a centaur (half man, half horse), from the Geometric Period, was found at Lefkandi.*

Classical Greek ways of life and thought have influenced much of the world. During the Classical Period, Athens was at the center of remarkable developments in architecture, sculpture, pottery, drama, and **philosophy**. The way that **city-states** were governed also changed during this period. Before, only the rich and powerful had an opportunity to rule. But from the late 6th century B.C.E., Athens and other city-states had begun to introduce **democracy**. This was a type of government in which many more adults were able to play an active part.

The Hellenistic Period

In the 5th century B.C.E., Athens was defeated by Sparta in the Peloponnesian War. But Sparta was soon defeated by another city-state, Thebes. In 338 B.C.E., Macedonia, ruled by King Philip II, grew strong and defeated Athens. Philip united Greece, and his son, Alexander the Great, went on to build a huge empire. During the Hellenistic Period, which began with Alexander's death in 323 B.C.E., Greek ways of life continued in much of the empire. Greece was taken over by the Romans in the 2nd century B.C.E.

The story of archaeology

To find out about ancient Greece, early historians looked mainly at written records, but later experts have increasingly used archaeology—the study of the past by examining ruins and old **artifacts**. The finds made by **archaeologists** are solid evidence of past events, so they can provide better information than an unreliable author. They may also show that an ancient text is basically correct.

▲ *When archaeologists excavate a site, they are looking for old objects that have become buried there. But sometimes objects are uncovered more unexpectedly. These ancient Greek pots were found when a new subway line was built in Athens in 2000.*

WHO WAS Pausanias?

Pausanias was a Greek historian in the 2nd century C.E., when Greece was under Roman rule. He was born in Turkey, but traveled around Greece examining ancient towns and villages. Then he returned home to write his "Guide to Greece." Pausanias designed his book for travelers of his own times. Since it was written when many buildings from the Greek Classical Period were still standing, the book helps modern archaeologists understand how sites once looked.

Many of the first **excavations**, in the 1700s, were carried out by rich men from England, France, and Germany, who were looking for works of art to take away to museums. However, in the early 1800s, English and French archaeologists made **surveys** of all the major Greek sites. In 1837, the Greek Archaeological Service was founded, and soon France, England, and other countries also set up archaeological organizations in Greece. The first major discoveries were made by German archaeologist Heinrich Schliemann in the 1870s at Mycenae.

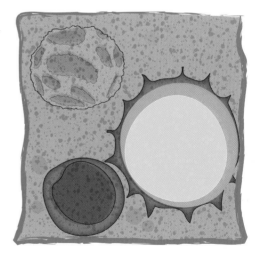

The way archaeologists work has changed over time. They have learned to excavate sites more thoroughly, and to use scientific techniques such as **radio-carbon dating** and pollen analysis. For years, Mycenaean and Classical sites were the most commonly excavated, but digs at the Hellenistic site of Vergina in the 1970s and the Geometric site of Lefkandi in the 1980s led to a growing interest in these other eras. Archaeologists today face many challenges, but they are still keen to discover more about the fascinating world of ancient Greece.

▲ *By analyzing pollen grains left in different layers of the soil, archaeologists can work out what crops were grown by Greek farmers in different periods.*

DID YOU KNOW? The people of ancient Greece called themselves Hellenes, not Greeks.

7

THE FIRST GREEKS

The first Greek-speaking people arrived in the land now known as Greece in about 2000 B.C.E. This was in the middle of the Bronze Age, when humans made tools and other objects from bronze and copper instead of the stone that they had used earlier. In time, the Greeks grew more powerful. By 1600 B.C.E., several rich, Greek-speaking kings ruled different areas of the land. Grand palaces were constructed to house each royal family, and cities gradually grew up around them. These cities had massive walls to defend them from attack.

▽ *The potter's wheel was probably introduced to Greece by the people who arrived in the Bronze Age. This pot was made at that time.*

Fantasy or Fact?

Homer's poem, "The Iliad," tells the story of Paris, a prince of Troy, who captured Helen, the wife of a Greek king named Menelaus. To punish Paris and bring Helen back, the Greeks fought a war against the Trojans (the people of Troy). Experts disagree about whether the poem describes real events. Some say that Homer wrote it in the 8th century B.C.E., long after the war was supposed to have taken place, so it is unlikely to be accurate. Other experts point out that Homer was retelling stories that Greeks had known for hundreds of years. Archaeology is helping to solve this puzzle.

More than 3,000 years later, in the 1800s, ruins from the largest of the cities, Mycenae, could still be clearly seen on the ground—but no one guessed what magnificent treasures lay hidden underneath.

Discovering Mycenae

One man in particular was responsible for uncovering the riches of Mycenae: Heinrich Schliemann. He wanted to dig in Mycenae in order to prove that stories told by the ancient Greek poet Homer were true. Homer's works described the Trojan War, which was fought by Mycenaeans and other Greeks against the people of Troy.

◁ Archaeologists excavating the palace at Mycenae and the royal tombs, called "Grave Circle A," have revealed a wealth of information about the early Greeks.

In the early 1870s, Schliemann excavated at Hissarlik in Turkey and showed that it could have been the city of Troy. Then, in 1874, he turned his attention to Mycenae. Over the following years, Schliemann uncovered and examined much of the city. His and later finds have enabled experts to understand the early period of Greek history, usually called the Mycenaean Period, better than ever before.

▽ Heinrich Schliemann and his wife, Sophie.

WHO WAS Heinrich Schliemann?

Heinrich Schliemann was born in Germany in 1822. He became fascinated by ancient Greece after he received a book of Greek legends as a Christmas present. Since his family was poor, he could not afford to train as a professional **archaeologist.** *So he became a* **merchant.** *By the time he was in his 40s, Schliemann was a millionaire. As a result, he was able to give up work and devote himself to his real love—the history of ancient Greece.*

A rich kingdom

Archaeology has shown that at Mycenae, kings ruled over a rich kingdom whose people were both warriors and **merchants**.

Shaft graves

Heinrich Schliemann excavated royal tombs in part of Mycenae known as Grave Circle A. They were all shaft graves, made by digging a passage (shaft) down from the surface. Bodies were placed at the bottom, along with objects known as **grave goods**. These included gold masks, jewelry, and many swords—signs of Mycenaean wealth and warlike nature. Another grave group, Circle B, excavated in the 1950s, revealed many more fine objects.

Fantasy or Fact?

When Schliemann picked up this gold mask, which had covered the face of one of the bodies in Grave Circle A, he cried: "I have gazed upon the face of Agamemnon." According to "The Iliad," Agamemnon was the king of Mycenae who led the Greeks to war against the Trojans. However, experts have shown that the mask dates from a period at least 300 years earlier than Agamemnon could have lived.

Off to war

One pot found at Mycenae has been named "The Warrior Vase" because it is decorated with paintings of soldiers and a woman waving them goodbye. The early Greek armor of the soldiers can be clearly seen.

Beehive tombs

In about 1500 B.C.E., the Mycenaeans stopped digging shaft graves for the royal dead and began to build domed tombs instead. These are called *tholos* (beehive) tombs because of their shape. The most splendid, the Treasury of Atreus, was excavated in the 1920s. The goods it once contained had been stolen, but experts could tell that the tomb had been richly decorated inside and out.

Archaeology Challenge

The Mycenaeans learned to write from the Minoans, a non-Greek people living on the island of Crete, with whom the Mycenaeans had strong links. Minoan writers used a **script** known as Linear A, but the Mycenaeans adapted it to produce a new script, Linear B. Some clay tablets with Linear B on them were found at Mycenae, and even more were discovered at Pylos, another city from Mycenaean times. In 1952, a young man named Michael Ventris and other experts **deciphered** Linear B. Linear A has yet to be deciphered.

A powerful palace

Many **archaeologists** have excavated Mycenae's palace, in the highest part of the city. Fire had destroyed much of the building in about 1200 B.C.E. But the experts could still see the layout and identify the remains of the courtyard and main area of the palace, called the *megaron*. This contained a porch, a hall, and a throne room with a central **hearth** and battle scenes on the walls.

Writings found on clay tablets at Mycenae have shown that the palace was not just a home for royal families. It was also a business center, where kings and officials controlled the buying and selling of items such as cloth, olive oil, and animals, in the city and surrounding countryside.

GOVERNMENT AND SOCIETY

By the late 8th century B.C.E., the Mycenaean kingdoms were a distant memory for Greeks. Now most people belonged to a *polis*—a self-governing **city-state**. At the heart of each was a heavily defended city that also controlled the nearby countryside.

▷ *The* **agora** *(marketplace) of the city-state of Athens is at the front of this picture. The hill towering above the city at the back is the* **Acropolis.**

Discovering Athens

Each city-state governed itself differently. Sparta, in southern Greece, was ruled by two kings and a council, but Athens, to the northeast, was much more typical. Like many other city-states, Athens was first controlled by a group of rich landowners called aristocrats. Then, in the 6th century B.C.E., the city was briefly governed by tyrants—men who had seized power illegally and ruled alone. The second tyrant, Hippias, was thrown out in 510 B.C.E. About two years later another man, Kleisthenes, introduced a new form of government, known as **democracy**. Democracy allowed far more people to participate, and made it harder for aristocrats to misuse their power.

WHO WAS Pericles?

When Kleisthenes introduced democracy, he divided the people of Athens into ten tribes. Each tribe elected its own leader, known as a strategos. Pericles was strategos of his tribe every year from 443 to 429 B.C.E. In this role, he had to speak at the assembly, a large outdoor gathering of men that formed an important part of Athenian government. His speeches were famous for their power.

In 480 B.C.E., Persian invaders destroyed the temples on the Acropolis. Between 447 and 438 B.C.E., Pericles organized the reconstruction of some of the buildings, and was responsible for building the Parthenon.

▽ *The Parthenon was a great temple dedicated to Athena, the patron goddess of Athens. Athena was also the goddess of wisdom and war.*

The *agora*

One of the busiest and most important places in ancient Athens was a large open area known as the *agora,* or marketplace. From the 6th century B.C.E., when democracy began, and especially during the Classical Period, the *agora* was largely reconstructed. Many of the new buildings, such as the council chamber and law courts, were used by government officials.

Historians have learned a lot about Athenian government from books by ancient Greeks, such as the **philosopher** Aristotle, but finds in the *agora* have revealed even more information.

Archaeologists from the American School of Classical Studies started digging there in 1931, and have unearthed not only public buildings, but also objects such as voting tokens that were used to carry out the everyday business of government.

Practical politics

The people who governed Athens in the era of **democracy** had much practical work to do—in particular, passing laws and punishing people who broke them. These tasks were carried out at *agora* buildings whose ruins were excavated in the 20th century.

The council

The main law-making body in Athens was the council, known as the *boule*. It contained 500 men, 50 from each of the city's 10 tribes. **Archaeologists** found the remains of a large building called the *bouleuterion*, where the *boule* met. Next to it they found the ruins of a circular structure, the *tholos*. This was where the 50 council members on permanent duty lived and ate their meals.

Fantasy or Fact?

Athenian democracy was limited. Greek men living in Athens who had been born elsewhere, foreigners, women, and the Greek and foreign slaves who worked for Athenian **citizens** *could not take part in debates or votes. However, some slaves did have a special role at the Athens assembly. If a citizen spoke for too long and refused to stop, it was a slave's job to pull him down from the platform called the bema. Very rarely, a slave could buy his freedom, become a citizen, and then take part in democratic government.*

Courts and juries

Archaeologists have excavated the ruins of several *agora* law courts. There, large juries of citizens—201 was the minimum number—listened carefully to legal cases. People accused of crimes did not have lawyers to represent them, so they had to speak for themselves. So, too, did the people who had accused them. After the speeches, the jury voted secretly by handing in small, circular tokens that looked like miniature spinning tops. A token with a hollow center meant "guilty," while a solid center meant "innocent." Many tokens have been unearthed.

The assembly

Laws prepared by the *boule* had to be approved by all the male citizens of Athens. Together, they formed the assembly. At first it met in the *agora*, but from the 5th century B.C.E., its members usually gathered on top of a hill, named the Pnyx. Several important finds have been made there, including the *bema* (rock platform) on which men stood to speak.

▲ *Remains at the Pnyx help archaeologists build a picture of the Athens assembly.*

▲ *The writing on this ostrakon says "Aristeides, son of Lysimachos."*

Ostraka

Every year, all the assembly members were asked if they thought any politician in Athens was trying to become an undemocratic tyrant. If the answer was yes, they had to scratch his name on a piece of broken pottery called an **ostrakon.** The politician whose name was carved on the most pieces had to leave the city for ten years. About 10,000 pieces of pottery used for this special vote have been discovered in the *agora* and other parts of Athens.

Planned cities

Most Greek cities had an *agora* where markets and government meetings were held. Many also had an **acropolis,** a high, heavily defended area where temples stood and **citizens** stayed in times of enemy attack. These were the places in which people lived their public lives. To find out how they lived in private, **archaeologists** have excavated ordinary houses in cities such as Olynthos.

Town planning

Athens grew up naturally over hundreds of years, and houses in many shapes were built almost anywhere they were needed. Archaeologists have excavated a few of these buildings, but not enough to give them a clear picture of home life in ancient Greece. By contrast, new cities built during the Classical Period, in Greece and the **colonies,** were more quickly constructed and carefully planned. The houses were all similar, and the streets were usually straight and crossed each other at right angles. **Excavations** at these planned **sites** have revealed much more.

◁ One example of planning in a Greek city can be seen at Priene, in modern-day Turkey. This picture shows the remains of the agora *and a straight street. The site was excavated by German archaeologists in the late 1800s.*

WHO WAS Hippodamus of Miletus?

Greek **philosophers,** such as Aristotle, had firm views about the layout of cities, but it was men like Hippodamus who did the practical work of planning new settlements. Hippodamus came from the city of Miletus in Asia Minor (modern-day Turkey) and worked during the 5th century B.C.E. Cities designed by Hippodamus usually had streets in a strict grid pattern, rows of identical houses, and a large central agora for public meetings. This style greatly influenced other city planners.

Discovering Olynthos

Olynthos is in the northern region of Chalkidike. In very ancient times, the people of the city lived in unplanned, irregular houses all over an area known as the South Hill. After Olynthos became a Greek city in 479 B.C.E., planners built a larger, grid-shaped settlement on the North Hill.

Olynthos was destroyed during a battle in 348 B.C.E., and its ruins were scarcely touched for more than 2,000 years. American archaeologists started to excavate there in the 1930s and found the ruins of more than 100 North Hill houses. Having completed their work, they covered up the remains, but recently Greek archaeologists have begun to excavate there again.

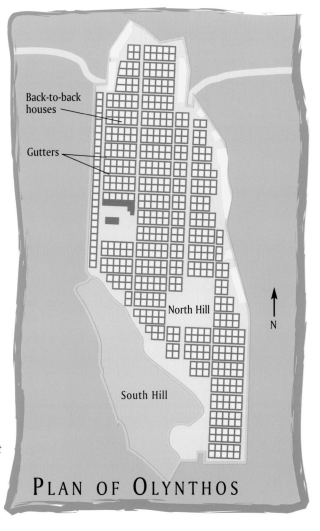

Back-to-back houses

Gutters

North Hill

N

South Hill

PLAN OF OLYNTHOS

▷ *With its houses in rigid straight lines, Olynthos looked dull, but archaeologists have shown that its people led busy home lives.*

Home life

Past and present **excavations** at Olynthos have provided some of the best evidence available about Classical Greek houses. Objects found in the houses, including bathtubs and spinning tools, have also provided clues about how people lived.

▷ *This **mosaic floor** found at Olynthos shows Bellerophon, a **hero** from Greek mythology. He is seated on his winged horse, Pegasus.*

Outside . . .

Nearly all the houses at Olynthos were in blocks of ten, arranged as two back-to-back rows of five. Each row faced a **gutter** into which people put their dirty water and other waste. Excavations showed that the house walls were made of mud bricks dried hard in the sun, and that roofs were covered with overlapping **terracotta** tiles. Archaeologists also found remains of stairs—evidence that some houses had an upper floor.

. . . and inside

Each house was built around a roofless courtyard, from which people could enter the rooms. There was always an *andron*, a dining room for men only. Usually the *andron* had low platforms around the edge, for couches on which men lay to eat. Often it was the only room in the house with a mosaic floor. These features made it possible to identify some of the dining rooms at Olynthos.

△ *Ancient Greek artists developed a type of pattern, called a meander pattern, that you can see around the border of this mosaic at Olynthos. It consists of lines that meet at right angles to form a continuous band.*

Women's world

While men were often out and about in the cities, Greek women spent most of their lives at home. They looked after children, cooked meals, and wove cloth.

The foods women prepared were simple. Breakfast was usually barley bread dipped in wine, and for lunch there was more bread with fruit or olives. At dinner, cooked vegetables, such as leeks, accompanied porridge or more bread. Occasionally there was meat, such as pork or fresh fish. Examination of the Olynthos houses has revealed some rooms that were probably kitchens. The rooms contain **hearths**, and pipes through which smoke from cooking fires traveled to the outside.

Items found for spinning and weaving wool include about 800 loom weights—clay pieces that were hung onto the end of the vertical threads in cloth as it was being woven. They kept the fabric tight and flat.

Fantasy or Fact?

Experts often emphasize that houses in planned cities were all the same. However, although they all had the same basic layout, every house at Olynthos was found to be slightly different from the others. Owners had changed the insides of the houses, either to make them more suitable for growing families or to make them look different. People moving into new houses today adapt them to suit themselves in just the same way.

Keeping clean

Few Olynthos houses had wells. Women had to fetch water for washing from public fountains in the city. About a third of the houses did have bathrooms, and archaeologists have even found some terracotta bathtubs. They were not long enough to lie down in—people had to bathe sitting up. Sinks and simple toilets have also been discovered. Most were not fixed to bathroom floors, but could be moved from place to place.

TRADE AND TRAVEL

From the 8th century B.C.E., many people were driven out of Greece by drought, **famine**, or overcrowding caused by population growth. Others left to set up trade links. As a result, Greek **colonies** and trading posts grew around the Mediterranean and Black Seas. Many colonies and posts were founded by people from the city of Corinth.

Discovering Corinth

Corinth's position made it an ideal trading center. It stood on a narrow strip of land at the top of the Peloponnese **peninsula** that makes up the southern part of Greece. This strip separated two areas of sea, one linking Greece with Western Europe, the other joining it to the East. Corinth had two ports, Kenchreai and Lechaion. In about the 6th century B.C.E., a stone haulway, named the Diolkos, was built. This allowed men to drag ships or cargo from port to port, instead of making the long sea journey around the peninsula. The Diolkos made Corinth even more accessible to trading ships.

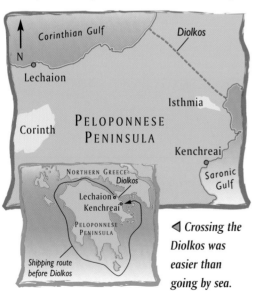

◁ Crossing the Diolkos was easier than going by sea.

▲ At Kenchreai, Corinth's eastern port, most ruins are Roman, but ancient books reveal how the Greek **site** looked. In the 2nd century C.E., Pausanias wrote that a statue of Poseidon, the Greek god of the sea, stood there. Corinthians worshiped him because they sailed across the sea to trade.

WHO WAS Archias?

Not everyone left Greece to find land and food, or to set up a trading business. Some political leaders were forced to leave by rivals fighting them for power. Other men were driven out because they had committed a crime. This was true of Archias, a **citizen** of Corinth, who was found guilty of murder. When he left in 734 B.C.E., he sailed west to the island of Sicily. He founded the Greek colony of Syracuse on its southeast coast. Like other Greek colonies, Syracuse continued to have links with its **mother-city,** Corinth. But Syracuse also became extremely rich and founded several of its own colonies elsewhere on the island.

In 44 B.C.E., Corinth became a Roman colony, where trade remained important. This means that Roman ruins now cover much of the site. However, **archaeologists** from the American School of Classical Studies and other organizations have still been able to excavate many ancient Greek remains. Buildings, pottery, and other goods have provided a great deal of information about trade in the ancient world.

▷ *Some Greek vases from Corinth had alphabetical writing on them. It helped archaeologists to know when the Greeks began to use this kind of writing.*

Archaeology Challenge

After the Mycenaean Period ended, the Greeks stopped using the Linear B **script**—in fact, they stopped writing altogether. Linear B was written using picture and other symbols, not an alphabet. However, as a result of the trade links that formed in the 8th century B.C.E., an alphabet did come to Greece. Experts think it was introduced to the Greeks by the Phoenicians, a trading people from the country now known as Lebanon. They are still trying to find out whether the Phoenicians brought the alphabet to Greece, or taught it to the Greeks in a place where they met for trade, such as Italy.

A trading city

Many archaeological finds made in Corinth show how it operated as a trading center, and the type of goods that its people bought and sold. Other finds simply reveal how trade made Corinth a wealthy city.

The haulway

Archaeologists have excavated large sections of the Diolkos haulway, which when complete was about 4.5 miles (7 kilometers) long. Their work showed that the haulway was paved with stones and had grooves on either side for the wheels of carts to run along. Experts believe that oxen were used to pull the carts, while men stood alongside to guide them and prevent loads from falling off.

City-center sites

Corinth was known for the riches it had gained through trade, and the buildings excavated there prove the city's wealth. Buildings include the South Stoa (covered walkway with columns) that in ancient Greek times housed 33 shops and restaurants on its two floors. Also important was the Temple of Apollo, the Greek god of light and music. It was first built in the 7th century B.C.E., and was the earliest Greek temple with a chamber for a god's statue. The remaining columns (left) are from a similar temple built about a century later.

Pottery and perfume

The Greeks were expert potters, whose style changed as time passed. In the 8th century B.C.E., the Corinthians developed a new type of pottery made from the yellow clay available near their city. On top they painted animals in black. Some animals were real, but imaginary beasts, such as **sphinxes,** were also included after the Corinthians had seen them on art in eastern trading areas, like Egypt.

Many pots in this new style were made especially for trade. Examples have been found not only in Corinth, the area where potters used to work, but also in Italy, Egypt, and Syria. Often the pots held perfume, which was also made in Corinth.

▽ *Greek coins found in Corinth showed Pegasus, a winged horse from Greek mythology.*

Archaeology Challenge

The city of Corinth controlled a nearby settlement known as Isthmia. Corinthians built a temple to the god Poseidon there in about 465 B.C.E. The temple's roof was made of **terracotta** tiles, and archaeologists have discovered several hundred of them. By making a few tiles themselves, they worked out that it would have taken seven people two years to make all the tiles for the roof.

Ships and sailing

Greek **merchants** used ships to carry trade goods to and from their homeland. Several underwater **archaeologists** have examined wrecks of these vessels to discover more about both them and their cargoes.

The Ulu Burun wreck

One ancient trading ship was found by a **sponge diver** in Ulu Burun, off the coast of Turkey, in 1982. Two years later, experts from the Institute of Nautical Archaeology in the Turkish city of Bodrum began to investigate. George Bass and his team found that most of the wooden ship had rotted, but much of its cargo had survived. The cargo included more than 350 copper ingots (bars), bronze daggers, gold jewelry, blue glass, hippopotamus ivory, and pottery.

▲ *An underwater archaeologist investigates a copper ingot at Ulu Burun.*

Dating the Ulu Burun wreck

Pottery found at Ulu Burun included items like this jug, made in Mycenae in about 1300 B.C.E., so the ship probably dates from that time. It is likely that the vessel was a Greek one, carrying treasures from lands such as Cyprus and Egypt to a Mycenaean palace. Wherever the ship came from, its contents prove the importance of trade in and around Greece during Bronze Age times.

The Giglio Island wreck

Underwater archaeologists have also found trading ships from later periods of Greek history. They include a wreck discovered at Giglio Island, off the west coast of Italy. Experts believe it sailed between Greece and Italy from the 8th to the 6th century B.C.E., when Corinth was a powerful trading center. Perfume bottles from Corinth were among the cargo, together with long, two-handled jars called *amphorae*. These were used to store liquids, such as wine and olive oil, two of ancient Greece's main **exports**.

Fantasy or Fact?

One Greek **myth** tells the story of Jason, who sailed a ship named the Argo to the Black Sea to find a golden sheep's **fleece.** Experts believe this tale may have developed from true stories of Greek trading trips to the Black Sea. To test the idea, explorer Tim Severin built a copy of an ancient Greek **merchant** ship with one sail and twenty oars. In 1984, he and his crew successfully sailed the ship across the 1,500 miles (2,400 kilometers) of sea between Greece and Georgia, a country on the shores of the Black Sea.

Ship shapes

By looking at wrecks and reading ancient books, experts have worked out what Greek trading ships, known as merchantmen, probably looked like. They were made of pinewood and measured about 100 feet (30 meters) from end to end. In the center, was a wooden mast with one rectangular **linen** sail hanging from it. If there was not enough wind to fill the sail, the ships could be rowed along. To steer them, the crew used two long oars at the back, as well as an underwater blade called a rudder. It was operated by turning a handle on the deck.

▷ *Here archaeologist George Bass is trying out a small model of a Greek trading ship to see how it sails.*

WAR AND WARRIORS

Greek **city-states** such as Athens and Sparta often fought among themselves, but the great foreign enemy of Greece was Persia. Greece and Persia clashed in a series of wars during the 5th century B.C.E.

▽ *The plain of Marathon lies at the edge of a bay 26 miles (42 kilometers) east of Athens.*

Discovering Marathon

One important battle between the Greeks and Persians took place on the plain of Marathon, east of Athens. Early in the 5th century B.C.E., Athenians had helped the Greeks living in Persia rebel against the Persian king, Darius I. So, in 490 B.C.E., Darius sent 25,000 Persian soldiers to Marathon to seek revenge. As they faced just 10,000 Greek soldiers, most from Athens, but a few from the more northern town of Plataia, it seemed likely that the Persians would succeed.

Greek general Miltiades had other ideas and devised a brilliant battle plan. He made his forces stretch out in a line, with the weakest in the center. This was to persuade the Persians, who could see the central group easily, that the Greek army was less strong than it really was.

EYEWITNESS

"... the Athenians ... were the first Greeks, so far as I know, to charge at a run, and the first who dared to look without flinching at Persian dress and the men who wore it."

(Herodotus [c. 485–425 B.C.E.] describing the events at Marathon in his "History")

Next Miltiades sent his men forward, before the Persians had a chance to begin their attack. The men in the center of the Greek line were overwhelmed, as Miltiades knew they would be. However, the two wings of his army were able to crush their enemies between them. More than 6,000 Persian soldiers lost their lives, but only about 200 Athenians were killed.

The victory over the Persians was so great and unexpected that the Greeks made buildings and sculptures to **commemorate** it in Athens and other cities. Evidence of the battle and the Greek triumph also remains at Marathon itself. Greek **archaeologists**, such as D. Philios, began to excavate the **site** during the late 1800s and their work, together with books by ancient writers such as Herodotus, has given historians a good understanding both of the battle and its results.

WHO WAS Pheidippides?

Miltiades realized that the Greeks needed help to defeat the Persians, and so he sent a runner named Pheidippides to Sparta, 100 miles (250 kilometers) to the southwest, to ask for assistance. The Spartans, though, were celebrating a religious festival and could not come. Pheidippides had to run back to Marathon with this bad news.

After the battle, a Greek soldier ran to Athens to proclaim the victory over the Persians. Having made the journey in his heavy armor, he gasped out the news, then died. His run is commemorated in the "marathons" held around the world every year and at the Olympic Games.

Land and sea battles

Finds at Marathon have taught experts about the battle there, but other **sites** and **artifacts** have given a more full picture of Greek warfare on land and at sea.

A mound and a memorial

Inside a 30-foot- (9-meter-) high tumulus (mound) at Marathon were the ashes of the Athenian soldiers who died there—192, according to Herodotus. Athenians who died in battle normally had their funerals in Athens. Greek historian Thucydides said that at Marathon, the soldiers were cremated and their ashes were buried where they fought, as a sign of their bravery.

Archaeologists also discovered a stele (memorial stone) near the mound. The Greek words on it said: "The Athenians fought at the front of the Greeks at Marathon, defeating the gold-bearing Persians and stealing their power." The stele is now kept in an Athens museum, but a copy has been placed where the original once stood.

The Greek army

Soldiers on horseback once made up the most important section of the Greek army. But from about the 8th century B.C.E., foot soldiers, called hoplites, began to play the leading role in battles. This change was mainly because a strong Greek middle class had begun to emerge, whose members could afford good armor and weapons. Before, most Greek soldiers had been high-class aristocrats who were wealthy enough to buy armor and horses. At Marathon, only about 300 Athenians rode horses.

Hoplites

The Chigi Vase, which was made in Corinth but discovered in Italy, shows hoplites carrying the round *hoplon* shields after which they were named. They are also wearing the main items of Greek armor—**crested** bronze helmets and metal breastplates. Finds of armor have proved the vase pictures to be realistic.

The vase shows hoplites fighting in large groups, called phalanxes, and using long spears. This was precisely what the soldiers did at Marathon.

▷ *This sculpture of oarsmen in a* trireme *comes from the Acropolis in Athens.*

EYEWITNESS

"Each [Greek] captain drove his ship straight against some other ship . . . when the mass of ships was crowded into the narrows . . . each crashed its bronze-faced beak [bronze ram] into another . . . and shattered its oars."

(Description of ships fighting in 480 B.C.E., from "The Persians," a play by Aeschylus)

Archaeology Challenge

The Greek navy fought in wooden ships called *triremes*. Archaeologists have learned about them by studying finds made at Piraeus, the port of Athens. The finds include a bronze **ram,** a naval warehouse where sails were kept, and many ship-sheds. *Triremes* were up to 115 feet (35 meters) long, with three rows of oars and one or two sails. Each *trireme* also had a bronze ram at the front to smash enemy ships.

RELIGION AND MYTHOLOGY

The Greeks believed in many gods and goddesses, each with a different role. The activities of these supernatural beings were related in stories called **myths** that developed in the Bronze Age, but were not written down until the 6th century B.C.E. Myths were also told about **heroes,** men who were half-human, half-god.

△ *According to Greek mythology, these mountains were the home of the gods.*

Discovering Olympia

The home of the twelve main Greek gods was thought to be Mount Olympus, a 9,571-foot- (2,917-meter-) high mountain in northern Greece. For this reason, the gods were often called the Olympians.

△ *Greek gods were thought of as people, with strong human feelings.*

The chief Olympian was Zeus, father of the gods, who ruled over the heavens. The five other male gods usually classed as Olympians included Zeus's brother Poseidon, who ruled the seas, and Apollo, the god of light and music. Among the six female Olympians were Hera, wife of Zeus and goddess of marriage, Aphrodite, goddess of love, and Athena, goddess of war and wisdom.

The gods were worshiped at many **sanctuaries**. One of the most important was Olympia, which stood on the Peloponnese **peninsula** to the south.

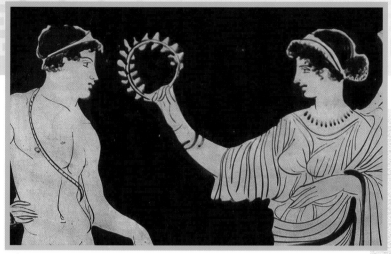

◁ This painting from a vase shows a woman presenting an Olympic winner with a wreath of olive leaves.

Various religious **rituals** took place at Olympia from very ancient times. It eventually became Greece's main center for the worship of Zeus. According to tradition, a festival and games in Zeus's honor were first held at Olympia in 776 B.C.E.

As time passed, Olympia grew increasingly powerful—and increasingly rich. Greeks from every **city-state** and many **colonies** came there to watch the sports contests, held every four years, and to discuss politics and business. Gradually, more and more buildings were constructed in and around the sanctuary.

Olympia is an exceptionally rich archaeological **site**—Pausanias wrote 41 chapters about it in his book. Since 1875, experts from the German Archaeological Institute have been digging there, and have uncovered a great variety of buildings, including temples and sport facilities that help to tell the long and complex story of its past.

Fantasy or Fact?

At first the games at Olympia contained only one event—a race to light the fire on the **altar** dedicated to Zeus. But eventually boxing, discus-throwing, chariot races, and many other activities were included in the five days of the contest. Only male athletes could take part, and in each event only the man who came first won a prize—a wreath of leaves taken from a sacred olive tree.

The fact that the prizes were not valuable has often led people to believe that the games were very pure, and that people competed only because they loved sports. In fact, cheating was common. People caught breaking rules were fined, and the bronze coins they paid the fines with were melted down to make statues of Zeus.

Temples and treasures

With its magnificent temples, multicultural visitors, and muscular athletes, Olympia during the games must have been a wonderful sight. The work of **archaeologists** can help us imagine what it was like, and understand how people worshiped the gods there.

◁ *According to Greek mythology, the* **hero** *Heracles carried out twelve labors (tasks), which included killing or capturing many animals and monsters. The eleventh labor, shown in this sculpture from the Temple of Zeus, was to fetch golden apples from a tree in the garden of the goddess Hera.*

The Temple of Zeus

The Temple of Zeus in the center of the **site** was completed in 457 B.C.E. From its remains, experts worked out that it had thirteen columns on each side and six across the front and back. Ancient writings reveal that the temple's central chamber contained a 43-foot- (13-meter-) high gold and ivory statue of Zeus. It was taken to Constantinople by Romans, but other sculptures have survived. Some show Heracles, the mythical hero and founder of the Olympic Games.

The main **rituals** in honor of Zeus were held at an open-air **altar** nearby. The altar was a tall structure, made from the ashes of offerings burned to please the god. Now, only a small mound of stones marks the site.

Treasuries and their treasures

Eleven buildings shaped like miniature temples were lined up along one side of the Olympia **sanctuary. Excavation** and research have shown that these were treasuries built to house gifts for the gods. Three treasuries were founded by Greek **city-states**, and the other eight belonged to Greek **colonies**, such as Syracuse.

Gifts for the gods were left in temples as well as treasuries, and archaeologists have found many examples at Olympia. They include a gold bowl, and a helmet presented by Miltiades, the general who led the Greeks to victory at Marathon.

Fantasy or Fact?

Some ancient Greek priests and priestesses claimed that they could contact the gods, and discover what would happen in the future. Many people brought questions to them, hoping that the gods would answer through their mouths. Both the answers given, and the places where the priests and priestesses worked, are known as oracles. There was an oracle at Olympia, but the most famous oracle in Greece was at Delphi. Its priestess was called the Pythia and claimed to speak on behalf of the god Apollo. She went into a trance to ask Apollo a question, then muttered his "answer." Afterward, attendants explained her words. The Pythia's services were popular, but her answers were vague. Like horoscopes, they could be understood in many ways.

▽ *There was an oracle at Delphi from at least the 8th century B.C.E. The priestess would wash here, in the Castalian Spring, before beginning her work.*

DRAMA, DANCE, AND MUSIC

The Greeks loved drama, dance, and music, and often performed them in honor of Dionysus, the god of wine and merrymaking. The earliest performances for Dionysus were called *dithyrambs,* and took the form of a hymn (a song praising the god) accompanied by dancing and by music played on pipes called *auloi.* The group of male performers—no women took part—were together known as a chorus.

As time passed, *dithyrambs* developed into drama. At first, plays were still sung and danced by a chorus, but in about 534 B.C.E., a man named Thespis wrote the first drama that included an individual actor who spoke his lines. Later Greek plays had parts for several actors, but the chorus always remained important.

△ *Actors in Greek plays wore masks to represent their characters and their feelings. This practice probably began during the 5th century B.C.E. The bronze mask above is from the Classical Period.*

Experts believe that Greek drama probably began in Athens. Every year a great festival called the *City Dionysia* was held there, and among its many events were four days of theatrical contests. From Athens, drama then spread all over Greece, and theaters were built in many cities.

▷ *This **terracotta mask** is from the Hellenistic Period.*

Discovering Epidaurus

One of the greatest Greek theaters stood at Epidaurus, on the Peloponnese **peninsula**. It was built between 330 and 320 B.C.E., and was part of a **sanctuary** where Asklepios, god of healing, was worshiped. Plays there were staged in honor of him, not Dionysus.

Worship of Asklepios continued at Epidaurus until the early 400s C.E. Then the **site** was closed by the Roman emperor Theodosius, who was a Christian and did not believe in the Greek gods. As the years passed, earth gradually covered the theater and other buildings. But in 1879, the Greek Archaeological Society, led by P. Kavvadias, began major **excavations** there. These continued until 1928, and there were several more digs later in the 20th century. Together, they taught experts a lot about the whole sanctuary and its magnificent theater.

Fantasy or Fact?

From early in the 5th century B.C.E., a major drama and sports festival in honor of Asklepios was held at Epidaurus every four years. However, what drew people to Epidaurus all year round was the hope that Asklepios would cure them of sickness or disability. People believed that if they slept in a building called the abaton, the god would heal them as they dreamed. During excavations there, **archaeologists** found two large stones on which people had scratched details of their cures. For example:

"Hermodikos of Lampsakos [a place in Turkey] was paralyzed. When he slept in the temple, the god healed him and ordered him to bring to the temple as large a stone as he could. The man brought the stone which now stands before the abaton."

At the theater

Seating and sound

The seating in the Epidaurus theater, as in most theaters in ancient Greece, was arranged in a sloping semi-circle, allowing everyone to see. **Archaeologists** found that there were 55 rows of seats. The 34 lower rows were from the original Greek building, which could hold about 6,000 people. The 21 upper rows were added when Greece was under Roman rule, providing room for a total audience of about 14,000.

Sound travels around this seating area, known as the *cavea*, very well. If someone stands at the bottom today and whispers or tears a piece of paper, people in the top row can hear it. It is likely that the voices of ancient Greek actors could be clearly heard, too.

Orchestra and altar

At the bottom of the seating is a circular area of earth surrounded by a strip of marble. Areas like this, known as orchestras, were where the chorus danced and sang. The English word "orchestra" comes from the Greek *orkheisthai* meaning "to dance." There is a circular stone on one side of the Epidaurus orchestra. It may be the base of an **altar** that once stood there.

WHO WAS Aeschylus?

There were three main types of Greek drama: **tragedies,** comedies, and plays in which men dressed as **satyrs.** Satyrs were mythical creatures who were half-human and half-animal. Aeschylus, who lived from about 525 to 455 B.C.E., was one of the greatest writers of tragedies. His plays included "The Persians," about the wars between Greece and Persia. He was also important to Greek theater in another way. It was probably Aeschylus who suggested that Greek actors should wear masks to indicate who they were and what they were feeling.

Stage and skene

The most damaged part of the Epidaurus theater lies behind the orchestra, but archaeologists have been able to work out how it originally looked. On either side of the orchestra circle were two passageways known as *paradoi.* Experts have **restored** and re-erected the gateways to these passageways (shown in the picture here), through which the chorus entered. Behind the orchestra are the remains of a raised stage known as a *proskenion.* This was where actors stood to make their speeches. At the back of the stage are the ruins of a building, the *skene.* Originally, a *skene* was a simple structure painted with pictures to show where a play was taking place. Later, more elaborate designs were introduced. From the stone foundations at Epidaurus, experts can tell that the *skene* there had pillars and a balcony at the back, and large rooms and colonnades (rows of columns) on the inside.

DID YOU KNOW? The front row at Epidaurus was for important people, so its seats had backs.

A NEW GREEK AGE

Most ancient Greeks looked down on Macedonia in northern Greece. Macedonians spoke Greek with such a strong accent that it was hard for non-Macedonians to understand them. There was even debate about whether Macedonians were Greeks at all. However, Macedonia's role began to change in 359 B.C.E. when King Philip II came to the throne.

Philip was a dynamic man and a skillful soldier. First, he took over all of northern Greece. Then, in 338 B.C.E., he fought alongside his troops and his son Alexander against the remaining independent **city-states**, led by Athens and Thebes. Victory in this battle, called the Battle of Chaironeia, gave him control over all of Greece. Philip did not enjoy his power for long, as he was **assassinated** in 336 B.C.E.

△ *These ivory carvings were found in the royal tombs at Vergina. They are thought to represent the faces of Philip II and his son, Alexander the Great.*

EYEWITNESS

"Before Zeus and all the gods, it is shameful and unworthy of you and of the history of Athens . . . to let all the rest of Greece fall into slavery."

(The politician Demosthenes in a speech to fellow Athenians about the threat from Macedonia and its ruler)

Discovering Vergina

Vergina is the modern name of Aigai, which for many years was the capital of Macedonia and the burial place of its kings. In the centuries after Philip's death, it was invaded and damaged by the Romans and others.

WHO WAS Manolis Andrónikos?

*Manolis Andrónikos was born in Turkey in 1919. He went to college in Thessaloniki, northern Greece, to study literature and then continued his studies at Oxford University in England. There he developed an interest in archaeology that stayed with him for life. In 1957, Andrónikos became Professor of Archaeology at the University of Thessaloniki, and it was in this role that he led the excavations at Vergina. The finds there brought him great fame and praise, and during his life he received several major awards. Andrónikos died in 1992, but his work is still remembered in museums and among **archaeologists** around the world.*

The Greek Archaeological Society excavated Vergina from the 1930s to the 1960s and made some fascinating finds. However, these finds did not prepare anyone for the treasures unearthed by Manolis Andrónikos and his team when they began another **excavation** in 1977. Andrónikos's excavations were designed to investigate the Great Tumulus, a 46-foot- (14-meter-) high earth mound in the royal burial ground. Inside the mound, he found three tombs whose dazzling contents have revealed much about Macedonian royal life.

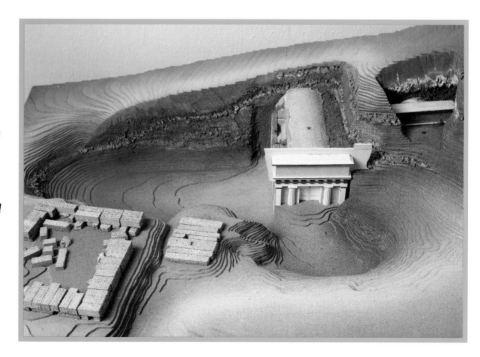

▷ *Andrónikos found three royal tombs at Vergina. This model shows how the tombs had been built inside a high earth mound. Excavations led archaeologists to believe that the central tomb was that of Philip II.*

Royal life

Two tombs

The tombs and other finds at Vergina showed **archaeologists** how some of the Macedonian royal family lived—and died. The first tomb had been looted by robbers, but still contained the bones of a man (probably a king), a woman, and a baby. The second tomb had never been opened before. To get in archaeologists removed the keystone (central stone) in the arched ceiling, then climbed down into the chamber.

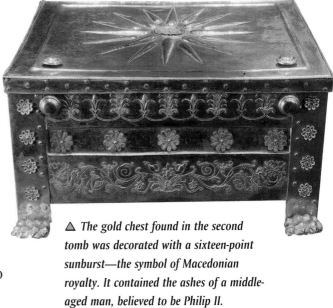

△ *The gold chest found in the second tomb was decorated with a sixteen-point sunburst—the symbol of Macedonian royalty. It contained the ashes of a middle-aged man, believed to be Philip II.*

Inside, they found two rooms. The inner room contained a gold chest decorated with a Sun symbol, the sign of the Macedonian royal family. There were also **grave goods**, including bronze armor and silver drinking pots. In the outer room were a second chest and more precious items.

Man and wife

To identify the people in the second tomb, archaeologists examined the contents of the gold chests. Inside the chest from the inner room were the cremated remains of a 35 to 55 year old man. Someone had wrapped the remains in a purple cloth, and placed a gold wreath on top. The skull showed the man had a facial injury.

Archaeology Challenge

Archaeologists asked British medical experts to examine the man's skull from the second tomb. The experts reconstructed the face to show how it probably looked when the man was alive. In doing so, they noticed that the man had a seriously damaged right eye. It was known that an arrow had struck Philip II in the eye during a battle, so this information made it more likely that the tomb belonged to him.

The remains in the other chest, also wrapped, belonged to a woman in her 20s. Most experts now believe that the man was Philip II, who died at age 46, and the woman was his last wife, Cleopatra.

The third tomb

Andrónikos also found a third tomb at Vergina. It contained the remains of a boy, possibly Philip's grandson, also named Alexander.

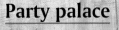

Party palace

Archaeologists have excavated a palace at Vergina, dating from about 300 B.C.E. It was built of mud brick and had a large porch at the front and a courtyard in the center. Many rooms leading from the courtyard were used for dining and entertaining male guests. Altogether, the palace dining rooms could hold about 300 people.

WHO WAS Alexander the Great?

*After Philip II was **assassinated,** his son Alexander became king. Alexander's military and leadership skills enabled him to defeat Persia, Greece's ancient enemy. He then continued his campaigns until he had built an empire that stretched all the way to India. Alexander died abroad in 323 B.C.E., and was not buried at Vergina. He may be shown in a painting of a hunting scene, though, that decorates the entrance to Philip's tomb. Some experts believe that the young man about to kill a lion in the picture may be Alexander.*

DID YOU KNOW? Alexander the Great was educated by the famous Greek philosopher, Aristotle.

ARCHAEOLOGY TODAY

Since serious archaeology began in Greece 200 years ago, some finds, such as the treasures at Mycenae, have been spectacular, while others, like the houses at Olynthos, were everyday. However, all the finds help experts understand how people lived and thought in ancient times. **Archaeologists** have used many techniques to aid them in **excavations**. For example, special diving skills have enabled archaeologists to recover the wrecks of ancient trading ships. Reconstruction techniques have allowed them to rebuild everything from powerful *trireme* warships to the faces of kings. In addition, archaeologists working in Greece have one advantage not shared by all excavators: except during the Dark Ages, Greeks could read and write. So, they have left texts behind that provide useful historical background to ancient Greek archaeology.

▽ *Columns like these at Pella are often the most visible, undamaged remains of ancient Greek buildings.*

Archaeologists continue to use all their skills in Greece as excavations continue. One major **site** where digs are still under way is Epidaurus. In the late 1990s, investigations discovered that a previously unidentified building, which dates from the 2nd century C.E., was a temple to three Egyptian gods (Osiris, Isis, and Arpocrates). Worship of the gods and goddesses of Egypt began in Greece during the Hellenistic Period, after Alexander the Great made Egypt a part of his empire. Worship of Egyptian gods continued when Greece was under Roman rule. Experts are now reconstructing the temple, using as much original stone as possible.

▷ Modern building work, as here in Athens, sometimes reveals archaeological remains. It may also threaten to destroy the remains or cover them up before they can be fully examined.

Pella, in northern Greece, is another site where archaeologists are still busy. Alexander the Great was born and educated in Pella, and in 410 B.C.E. it became the capital of Macedonia. Experts are now excavating the ruins of the palace in Pella, built to rival the royal homes in Vergina.

Athenian arguments

As there are so many important ruins in Athens, archaeological work there never stops. In recent times, a great deal of **restoration** work has been done on and around the **Acropolis**. Part of this work was to build a museum to house marble sculptures from the Parthenon. To make room for the new museum, builders had to excavate ancient remains, and many archaeologists objected strongly to this.

A lasting legacy

Archaeology in Greece has revealed a great deal about the ancient Greeks, and has also taught experts much about the Western world today. Many modern activities, from democratic government to theatrical performances, are based on the ideas of men and women who lived in Greece more than 2,000 years ago. For this reason alone, our interest in their lives is likely to continue.

TIMELINE OF ANCIENT GREECE

Experts divide the history of ancient Greece into five main periods: the Mycenaean Period (about 1600–1100 B.C.E.), the Dark Ages or Geometric Period (1100–750 B.C.E.), the Archaic Period (750–480 B.C.E.), the Classical Period (479–338 B.C.E.), and the Hellenistic Period (336–146 B.C.E.).

B.C.E.

About 2000

The first Greek-speaking people move into the land of Greece, during the period of history known as the Bronze Age.

The non-Greek Minoan civilization develops on the island of Crete and eventually develops trade and other links with Mycenae.

About 1600

Beginning of the Mycenaean Period in Greece. Rich kingdoms develop in Mycenae and other Greek cities such as Pylos.

About 1450

The palaces of the Minoan civilization are destroyed, possibly by the Mycenaeans. Many Mycenaeans then settle on Crete, reconstruct the great palace of Knossos, and build a strong trade network.

About 1250

Traditional date of the Trojan War between Greece and Troy.

About 1200

All the major Mycenaean sites are destroyed, probably as a result of both enemy attacks and earthquakes, and the civilization declines.

About 1100

The Mycenaean Period comes to an end and the Dark Ages, also known as the Geometric Period, begin.

From about 850

Life of the Greek writer Homer, whose great works "The Iliad" and the "Odyssey" describe the Trojan War.

8th century

Greeks start to found **colonies** around the coasts of the Mediterranean and the Black Seas.

An alphabet is introduced to Greece by the Phoenicians.

750

City-states begin to develop in Greece and the Archaic Period begins.

776

Traditional date of the first games at Olympia.

About 6th century

Diolkos haulway is built in Corinth.

Greek **myths** are first written down.

546

Peisistratos becomes the first tyrant of Athens.

527

Hippias, the son of Peisistratos, becomes the second tyrant of Athens.

510

Hippias is forced from power and civil war follows.

508

Athens begins to introduce a limited form of **democracy**. Athenians are divided into ten tribes.

490

The Persian Wars begin when the Persian emperor, Darius, tries to invade Greece. The Persians are defeated at the Battle of Marathon.

480

Persians invade Athens and destroy the temples on the **Acropolis.**

Persians are defeated at the Battle of Salamis, which takes place at sea.

479

The Persians are decisively defeated at the Battle of Plataia and the Classical Period begins.

From about 460

The leading statesman Pericles oversees the rebuilding of Athens after the Persian invasion. Among the major building projects is the great Parthenon temple on the Acropolis.

449

The Persian Wars come to an end when a peace treaty is signed.

431–404

The people of Athens and Sparta fight each other in the Peloponnesian War. The two city-states had long been enemies, partly because Spartans were jealous of Athenian power. War finally broke out between them after they supported different sides in another war.

359

Philip II becomes king of Macedonia.

338

Philip II defeats Athens and other city-states at the Battle of Chaironeia. He then becomes ruler of Greece and the Classical Period ends.

336

Philip II is **assassinated**. He is succeeded by his son, Alexander the Great.

323

Alexander the Great dies in Babylon after building a great empire that stretches all the way to India. His empire is divided into four parts, then into three. The Hellenistic Period begins.

146

Direct Roman rule over Greece begins.

TIMELINE OF GREEK ARCHAEOLOGY

C.E.

Early 1800s

English and French **archaeologists survey** all the major **sites** of ancient Greece.

1837

The Greek Archaeological Service is founded. Soon French, British, and other national archaeological organizations are set up.

Early 1870s

German archaeologist Heinrich Schliemann excavates Hissarlik in Turkey, the possible site of Troy.

1874

Schliemann begins **excavations** at Mycenae.

1875

The German Archaeological Institute begins excavations at Olympia.

1879

The Greek Archaeological Society, led by P. Kavvadias, begins major excavations at Epidaurus.

1884

Greek archaeologist D. Philios leads the first excavations at Marathon.

1892

French archaeologists begin excavations at Delphi.

1900

British archaeologist Sir Arthur Evans begins work at the site of Knossos, a Minoan palace on the island of Crete. He finds the first known examples of Linear A and Linear B **script**.

1920s

The treasury of Atreus is excavated at Mycenae.

1930s

American archaeologists begin to excavate the city of Olynthos.

The Greek Archaeological Society begins to excavate at Vergina.

1931

Archaeologists from the American School of Classical Studies begin to excavate the *agora* in Athens.

1950s

The Circle B group of graves is excavated at Mycenae.

1952

Michael Ventris and other scholars complete the **deciphering** of Linear B.

1977–78

Greek archaeologist Manolis Andrónikos excavates the Great Tumulus (mound) at Vergina and unearths what may be King Philip II of Macedonia's tomb.

1980s

The British School of Archaeology excavates the Geometric Period site of Lefkandi on the island of Euboia.

1982

The Ulu Burun wreck is discovered off the coast of Turkey.

1984

George Bass and other experts from the Institute of Nautical Archaeology in Bodrum begin to investigate the Ulu Burun wreck.

Explorer Tim Severin sails a copy of an ancient Greek **merchant** ship from Greece to Georgia, on the Black Sea.

1990s

New excavations begin at Epidaurus.

21st century

Excavations continue at Athens, Epidaurus, Pella, and many other sites.
Linear A script has yet to be deciphered.

45

GLOSSARY

acropolis

high, heavily defended area in any ancient Greek city-state. The term comes from two Greek words, *acro* ("topmost") and *polis* ("city"). When the word is written with a capital A, it means the high, heavily defended area in Athens on which the Parthenon temple stands.

agora

large open area in a Greek city for markets and public meetings

altar

stone, table, or other structure where priests held religious ceremonies and on which offerings to the gods were burned

archaeologist

person who studies the past by examining and scientifically analyzing old objects and ruins

artifact

object made by people, such as a tool or an ornament. Archaeologists often use the word "artifact" to describe an object they find that was made by people in past times.

assassinate

murder. The word "assassinate" is often used when a victim is an important person and has been killed as part of a political plan.

citizen

free man living in the city-state where he was born, and with full rights to take part in its government. Women and slaves could not be citizens. A free man was sometimes allowed to become a citizen of a city-state to which he had moved.

city-state

independent city that governed itself and the surrounding countryside

colony

city or state founded and occupied by people from another city or state. At first, Greek colonies were often ruled by the state from which their settlers came, but many soon became independent and self-governing.

commemorate

remember and honor a person or event from the past, for example by building a statue

crest

line of upright feathers, fur, or other decoration, from front to back on a helmet

decipher

work out the meaning of; decode

democracy

type of government in which many people are able to participate. The term comes from two Greek words, *demos* ("people") and *kratos* ("power"). In ancient Greece, every citizen was able to take part in government except for women, slaves, and foreigners.

excavation

process of excavating, that is digging up a building or area of land in order to look for ancient objects, ruins, or other evidence of the past

export

object that is made in one country, then sold in another

famine

severe shortage of food, sometimes causing many deaths. Famines often happen if crops have died, or if the population has grown so fast that there is not enough food for everyone.

fleece

wool coat of a sheep

grave good

object buried with a body in a grave. They are often precious items that the person owned when alive and wanted to keep with him or her after death.

gutter

narrow channel at the side or in the middle of a road, designed to allow water and other waste to flow away

hearth

fireplace, especially one that is on the floor in the middle of a room

hero

any of several male characters from Greek mythology who bravely carry out dangerous tasks. Many heroes had one parent who was a god and one who was a human.

linen

fabric made from the stems of flax, a blue-flowered plant

merchant

person whose job is to buy and sell goods

mosaic

floor, wall, or other decoration whose pictures and patterns are made from many tiny pieces of colored glass or stone

mother-city

city or state from which the settlers in a colony originally came

myth

tale about gods, heroes, or other superhuman creatures. Ancient myths often set out to explain how the world began, why dramatic natural events (i.e. thunderstorms) happen, and why people behave as they do.

peninsula

area of land that sticks out into the sea so that it is surrounded by water on three sides

philosopher

person who studied and often also taught philosophy, a word meaning "love of wisdom." Ancient Greek philosophy included many forms of knowledge, like science. Now Greek philosophers, such as Socrates, are remembered most for their ideas about human behavior and politics.

radio-carbon dating

way of discovering the age of some objects by measuring the amount of a substance, called carbon, that they contain. It works because plants and animals absorb a special type of carbon, Carbon-14, from the air when they are alive. When they die, this carbon decays at a known rate. So, the amount present in a piece of wood, bone, or other material that was once part of a plant or animal reveals how old the material is.

ram

pointed piece of bronze or other material attached to the front of a ship; designed to make holes in enemy ships

restoration

rebuilding and repairing an ancient structure in order to return it to its original state

ritual

special set of activities carried out in a fixed order, like a religious ceremony

sanctuary

holy place where religious ceremonies are held. Ancient Greek sanctuaries included huge temples, simple stone altars set up outside, and natural features (such as springs or rocks).

satyr

mythological character who is a mixture of man and goat (or horse)

script

set of letters, characters, or other symbols used to write a language

site

piece of land, especially one used for a particular purpose such as an archaeological excavation

sphinx

creature from Egyptian myths, with a lion's body and a man's head

sponge diver

person who dives to find sponges, simple sea creatures whose light, flexible skeletons are full of holes and can be used to wash the skin

survey

detailed investigation of a building or piece of land. It often includes taking measurements so that a map or other record can be created.

terracotta

baked clay

tholos

any of various circular buildings in ancient Greece. The word is used particularly to describe the beehive-shaped tombs found at Mycenae, but was also the name of the place in the Athenian *agora* where council members met to eat.

tragedy

play in which the main character, often a hero or other important person, faces a difficult choice about how to behave. Eventually the weaknesses of his character lead to disaster.

FURTHER READING

Chrisp, Peter. *A Greek Theater.* Chicago: Raintree, 2001.

Crosher, Judith. (Technology in the Time of) *Ancient Greece.* Chicago: Raintree, 1998.

Denti, Mario. *Classical Athens.* Chicago: Raintree, 2001.

Devereux, Paul. *Archaeology: The Study of Our Past.* Milwaukee: Gareth Stevens, 2002.

Hicks, Peter. *Ancient Greece.* Chicago: Raintree, 2000.

Middleton, Hayden. *Ancient Greek War and Weapons.* Chicago: Heinemann Library, 2002.

Orna-Ornstein, John. *Archaeology: Discovering the Past.* New York: Oxford University Press, 2002.

Shuter, Jane. *The Acropolis.* Chicago: Heinemann Library, 2000.